Islamic Geometric Coloring Book

Islamic Geometric Coloring Book

This Book contains twenty geometric patterns of some of the most famous and beautiful Islamic art and architecture. This relaxing coloring book is appropriate for all ages and levels and may be used for introducing the Islamic Art.

All Rights Reserved
Dalabeh©2020

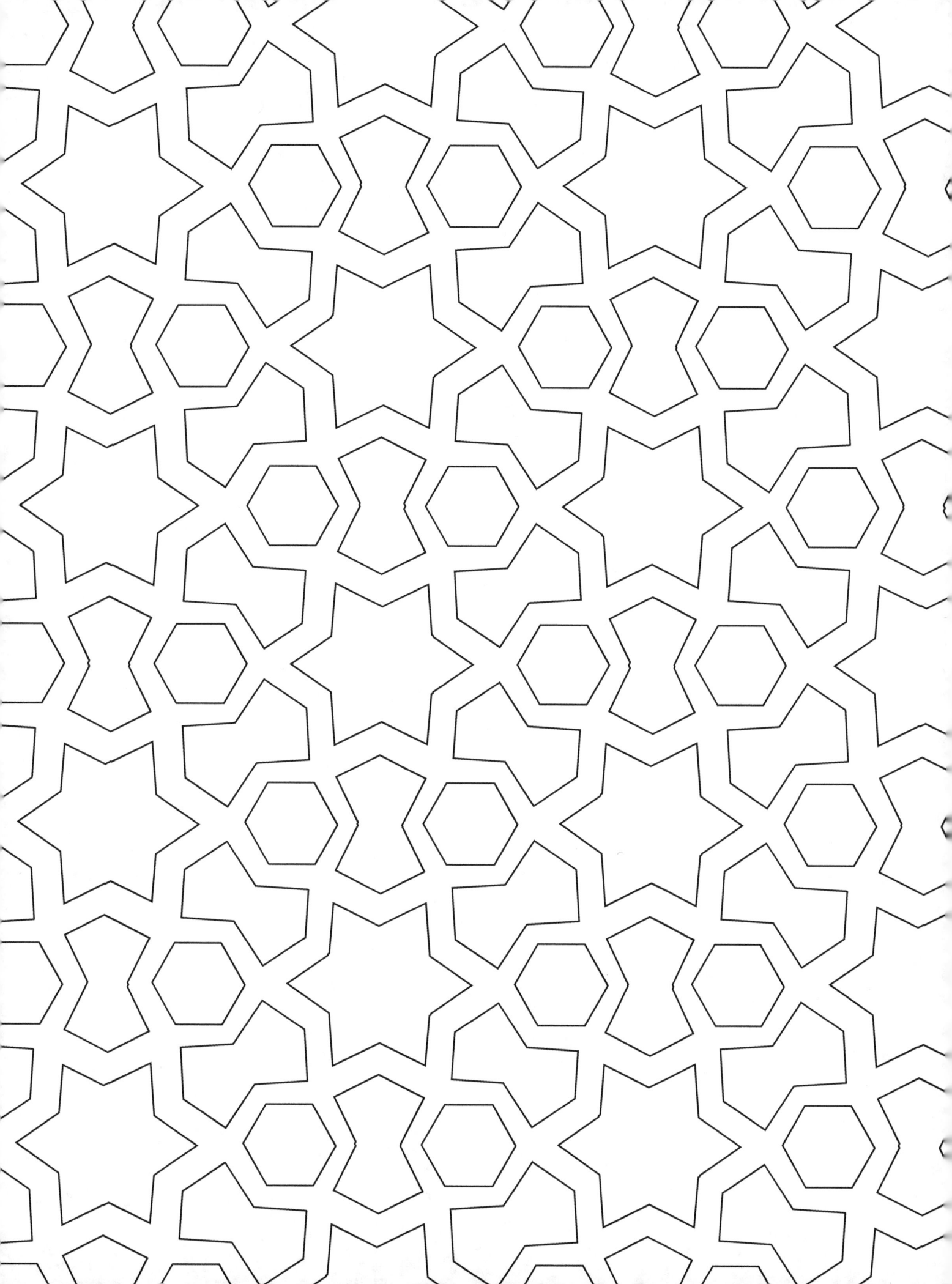

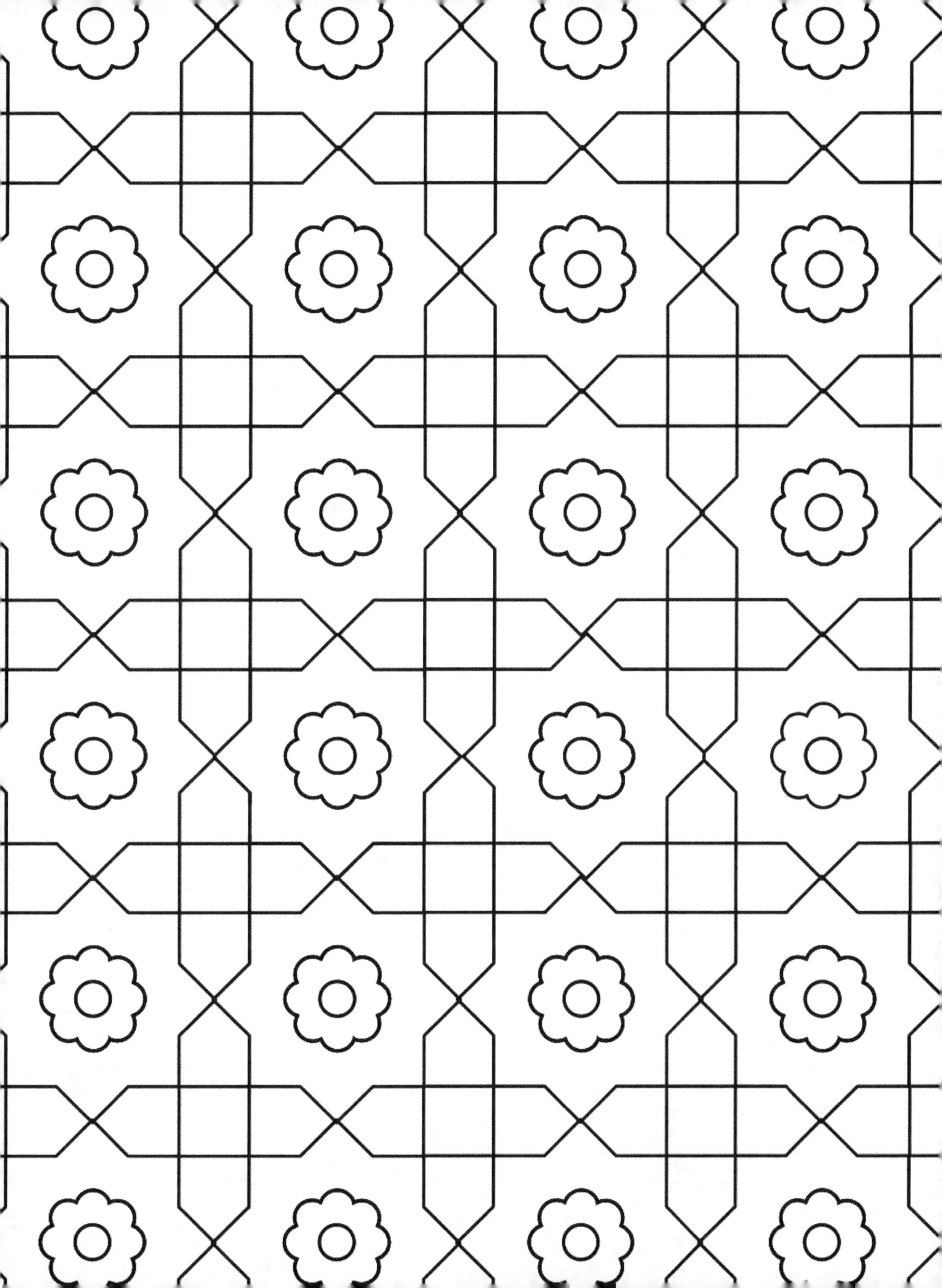

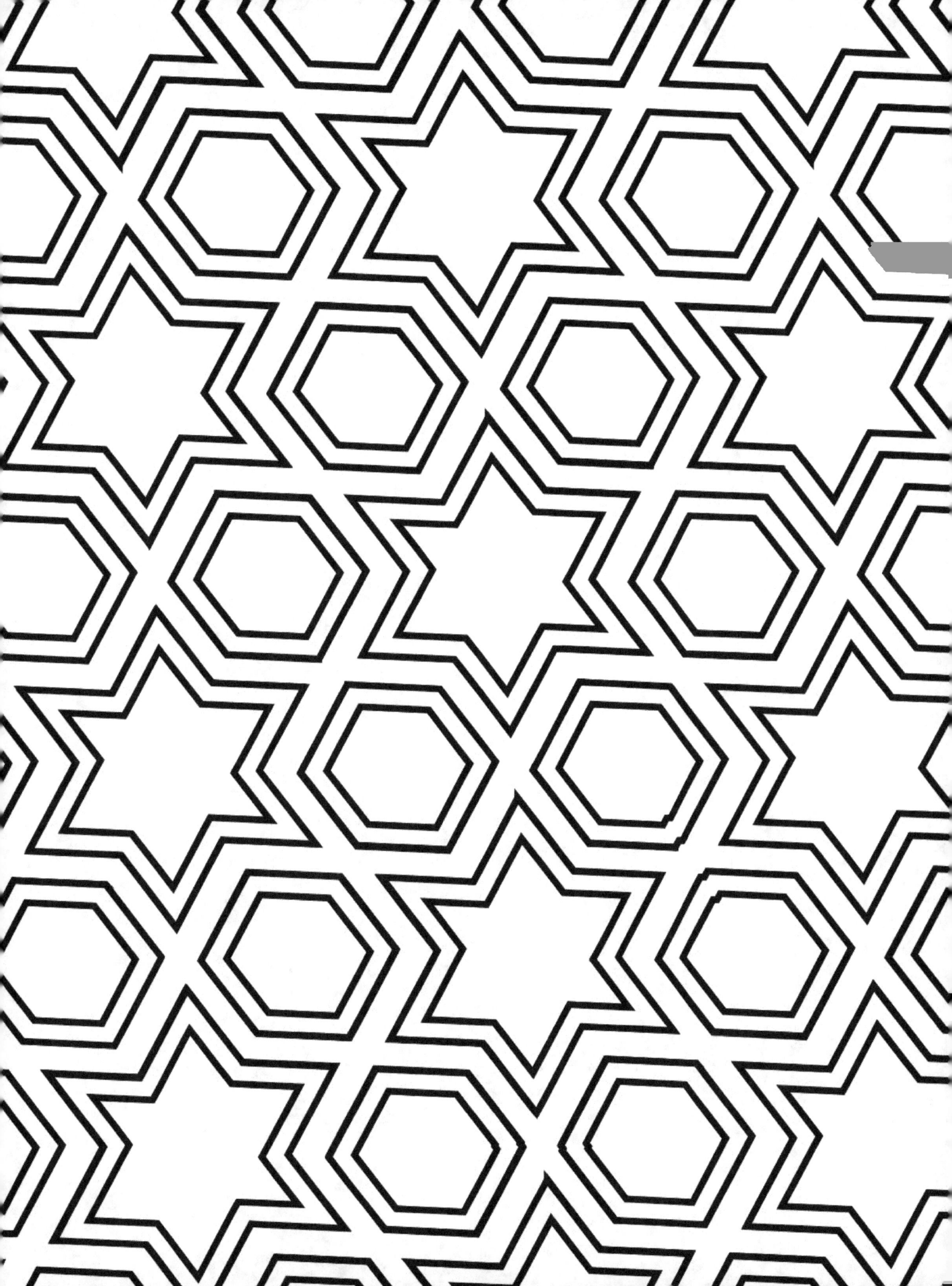

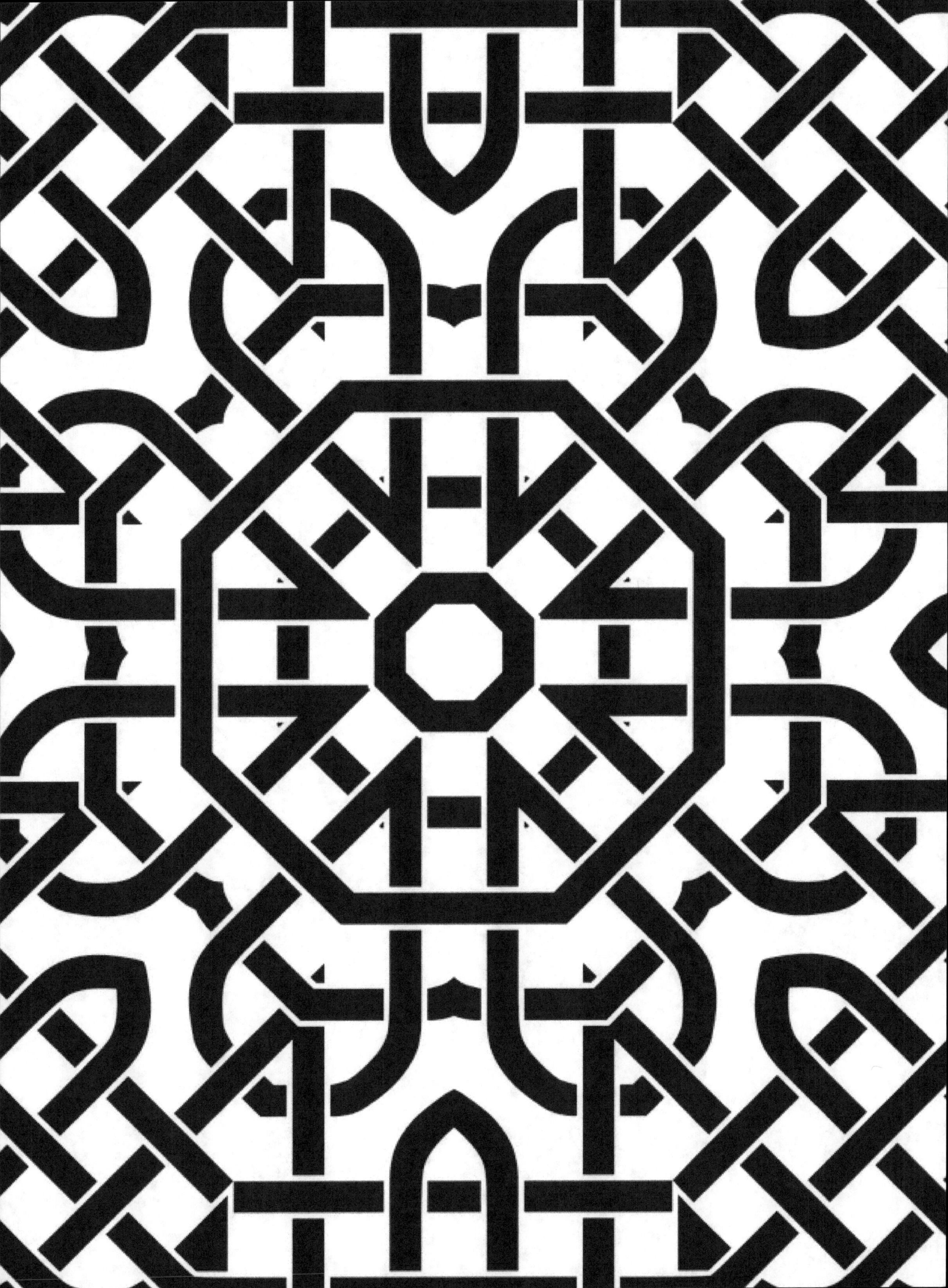

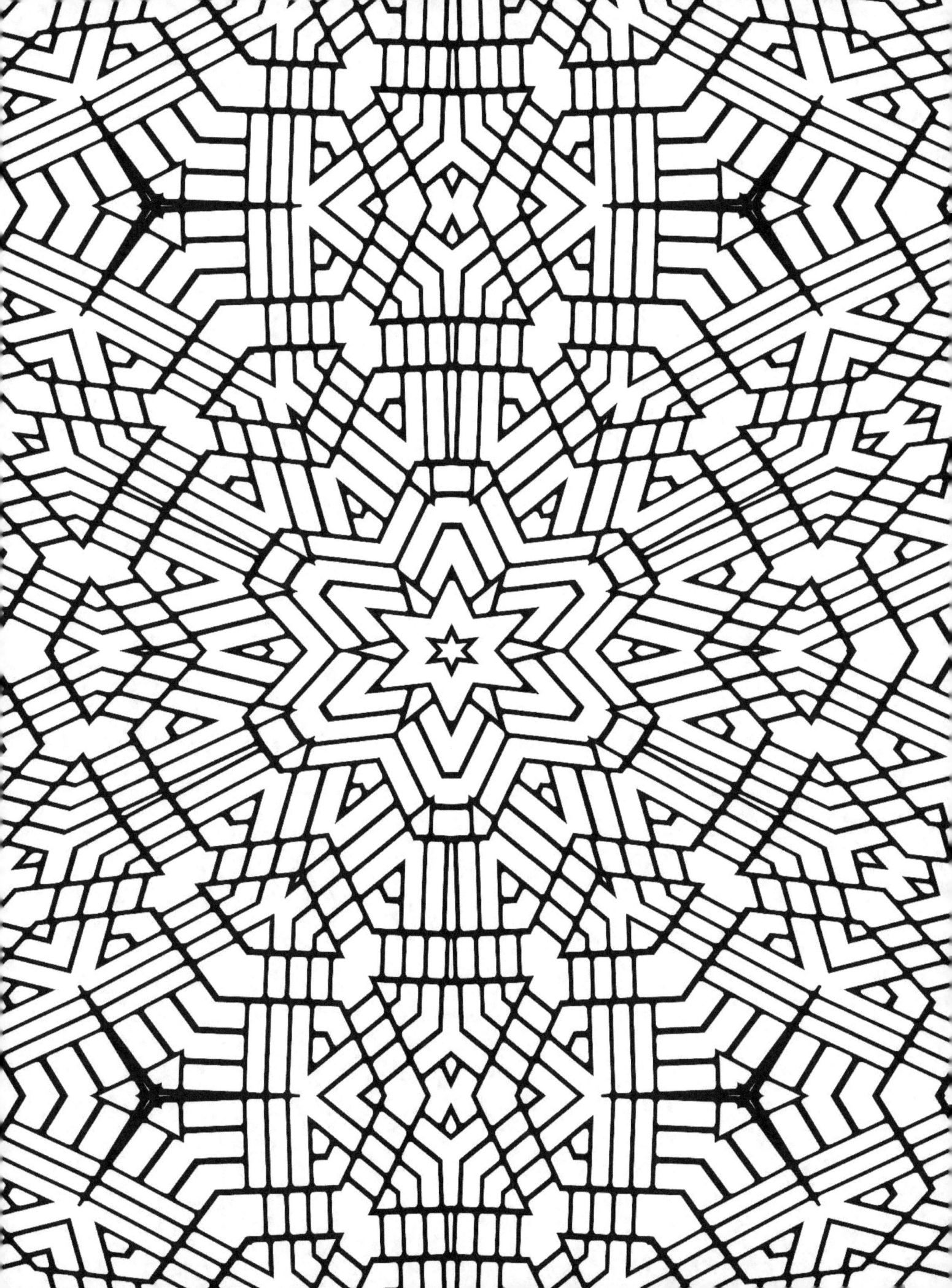

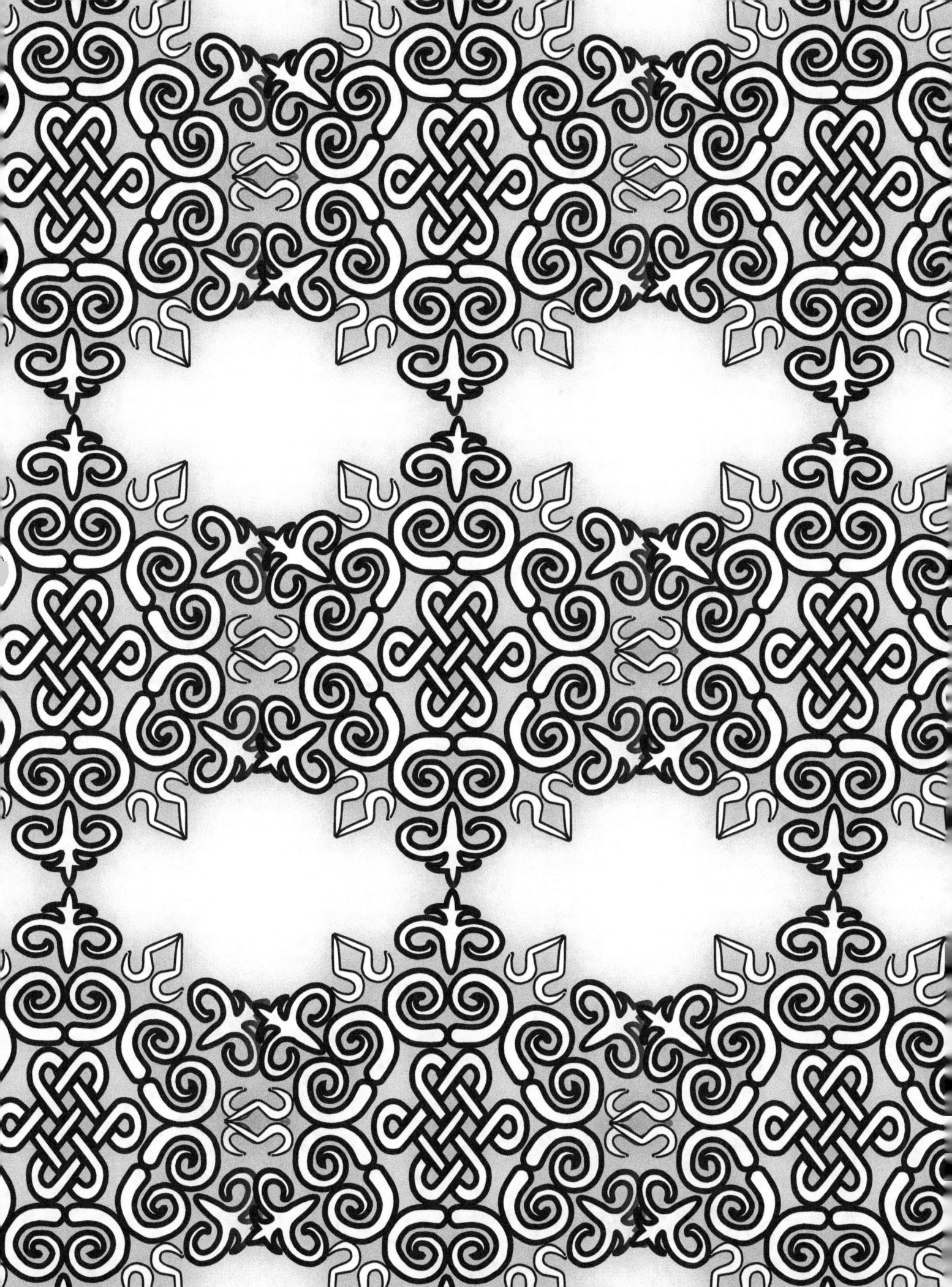

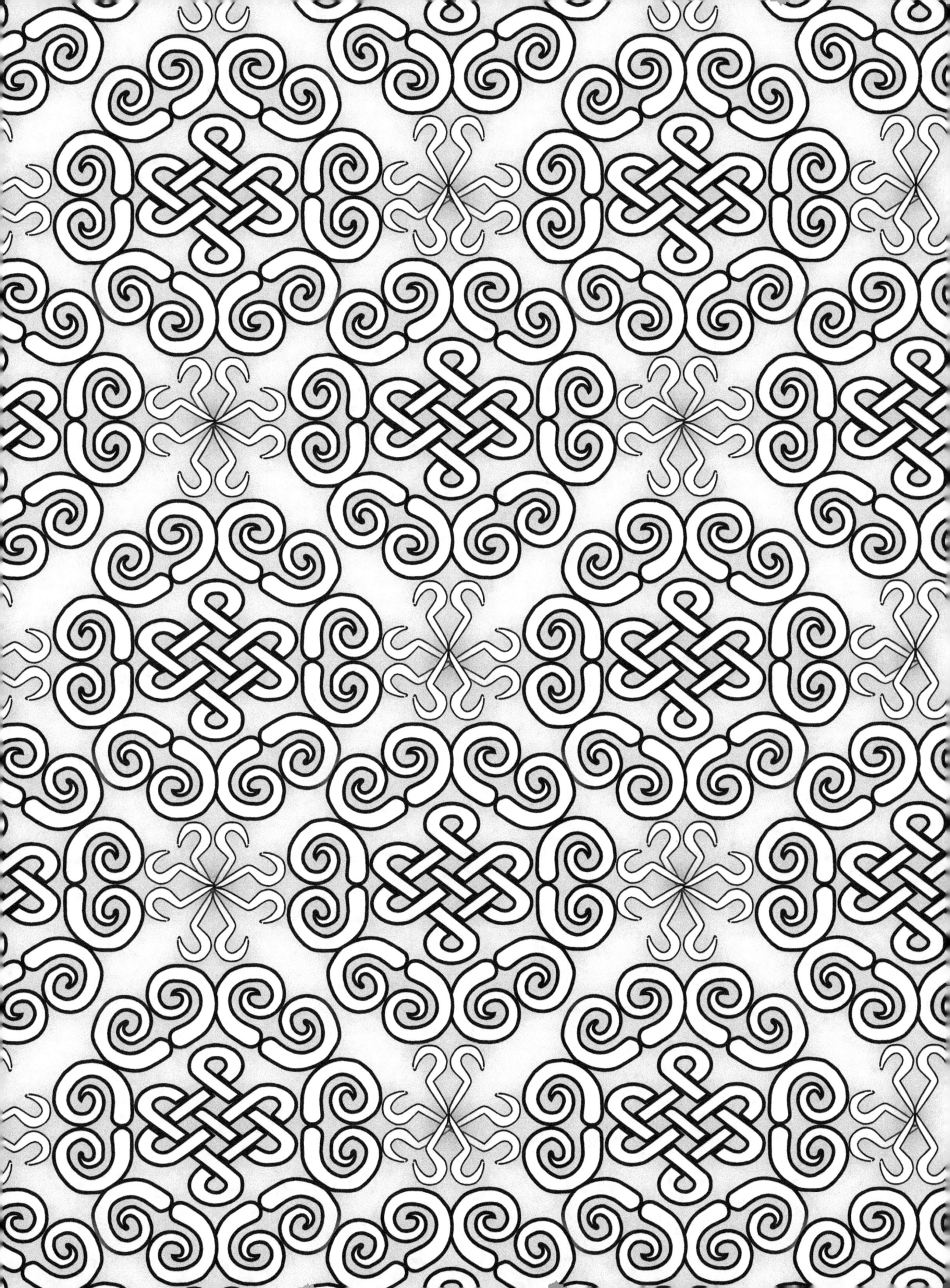

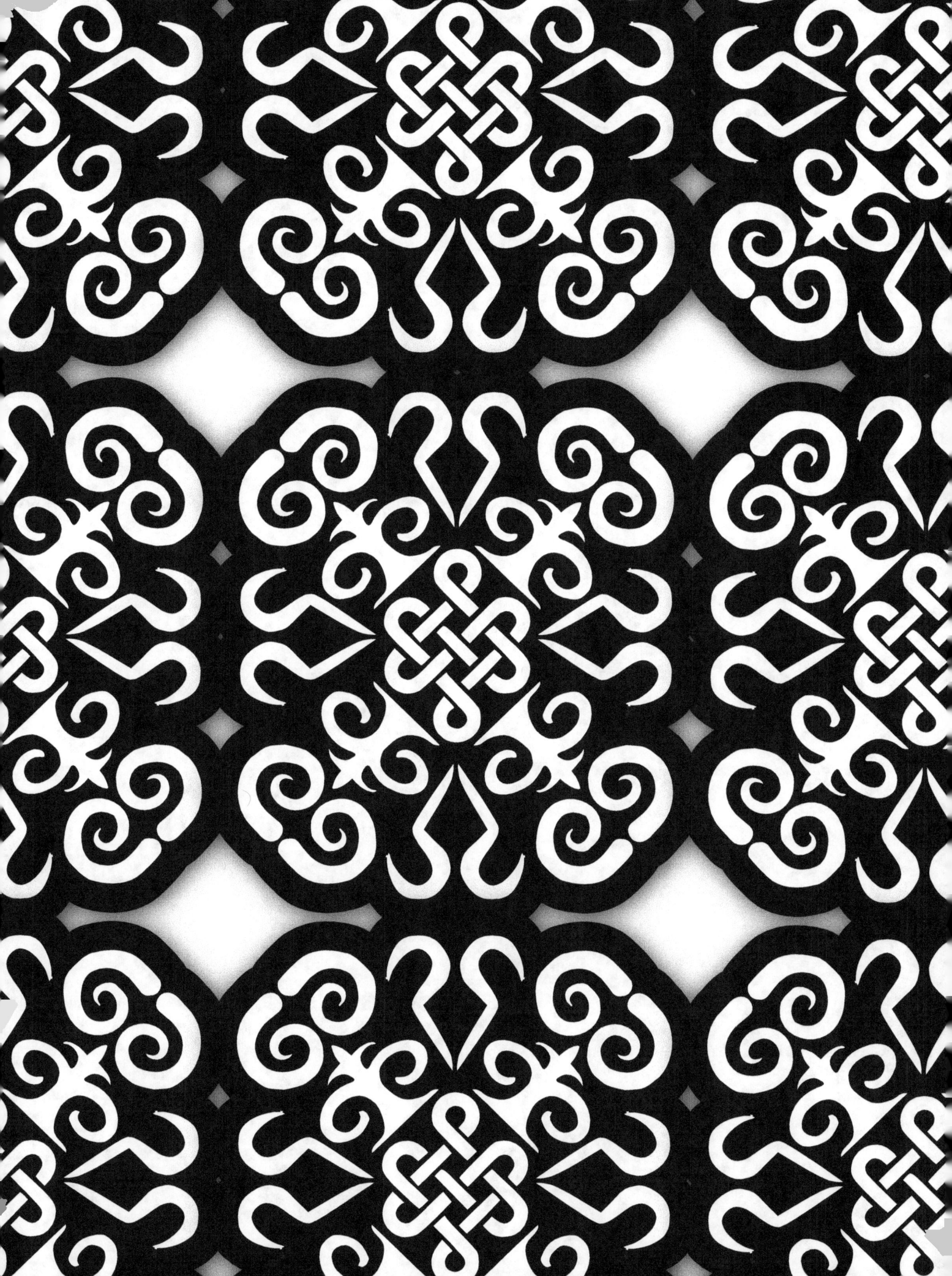

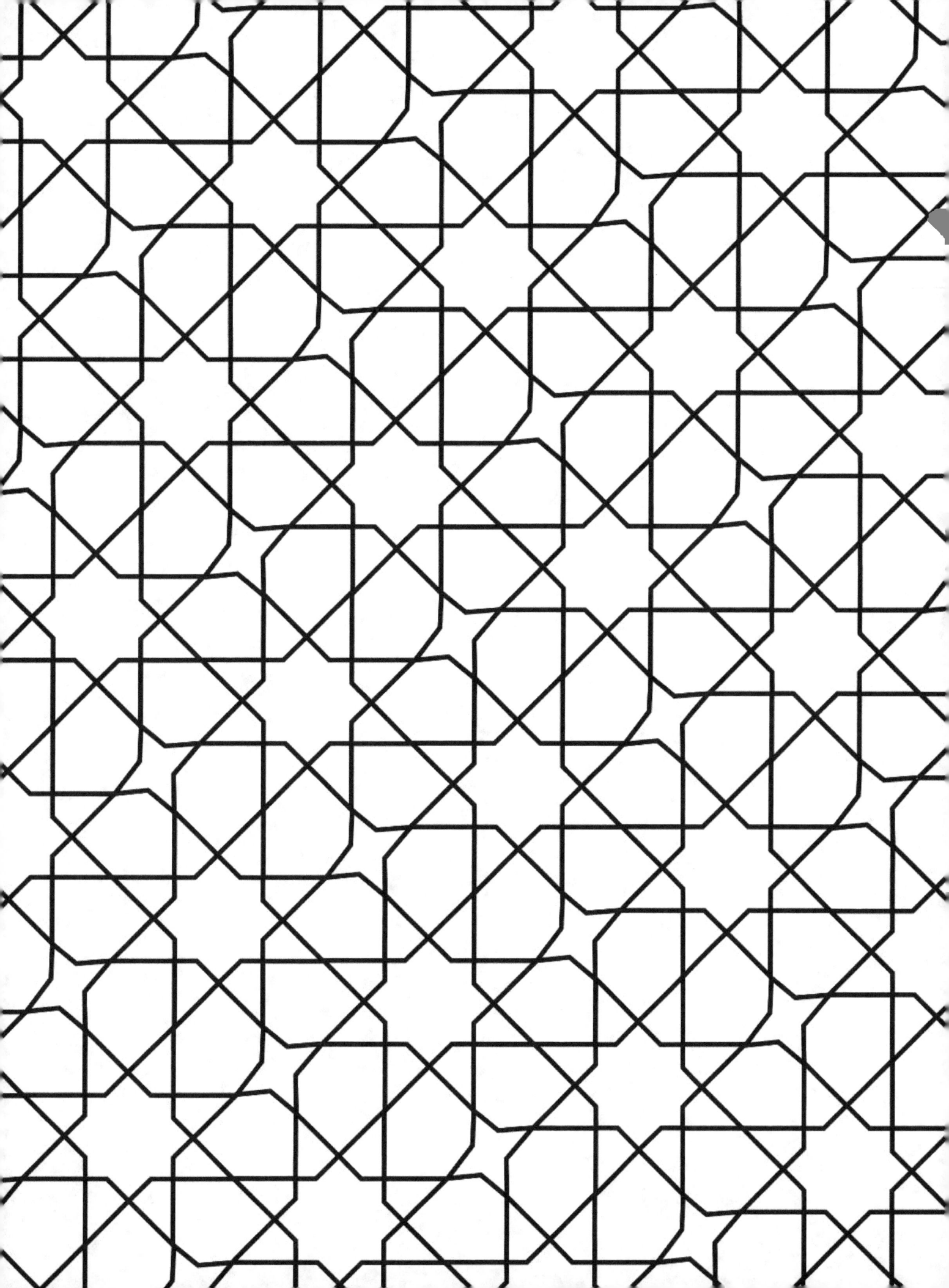

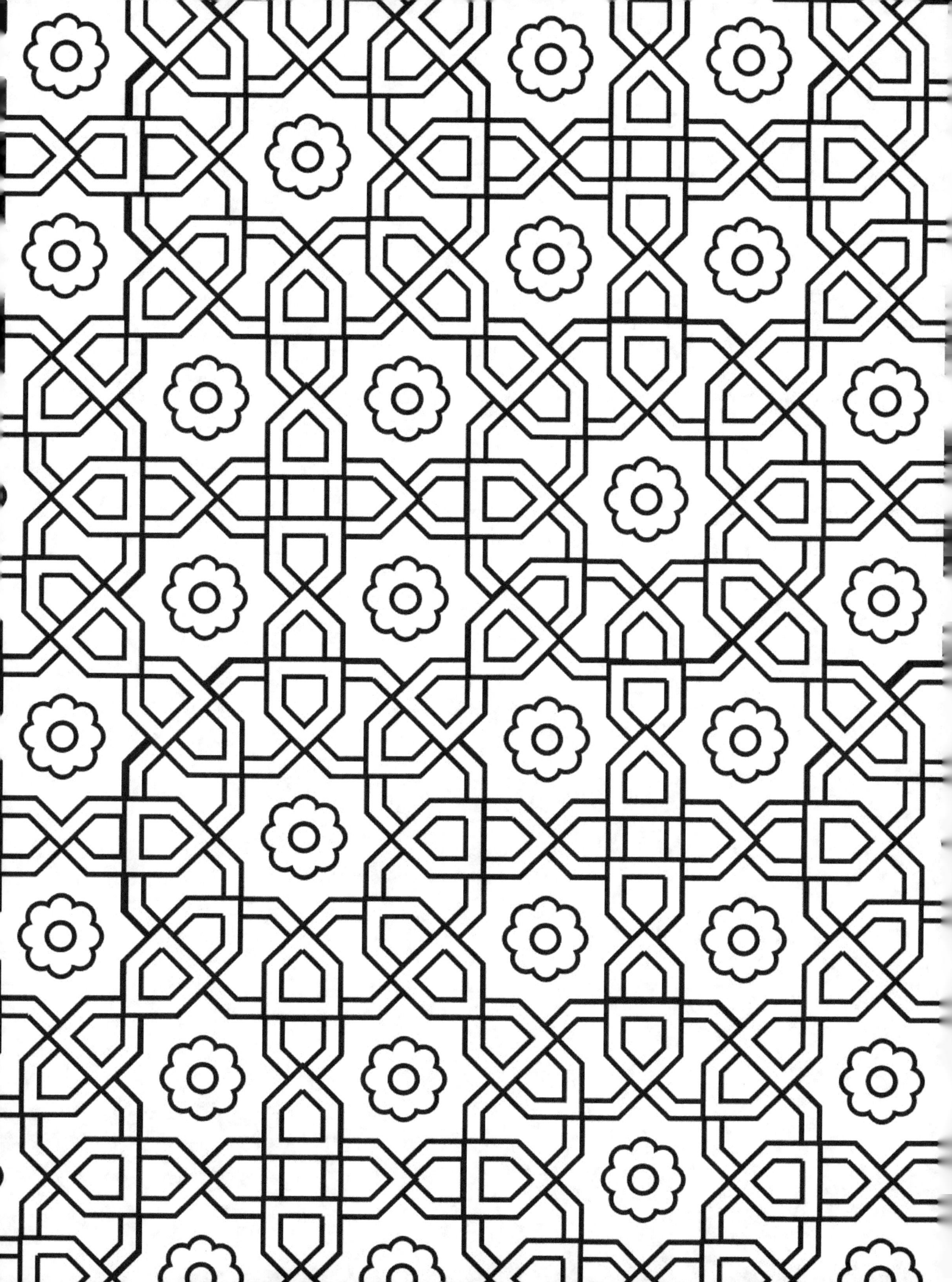

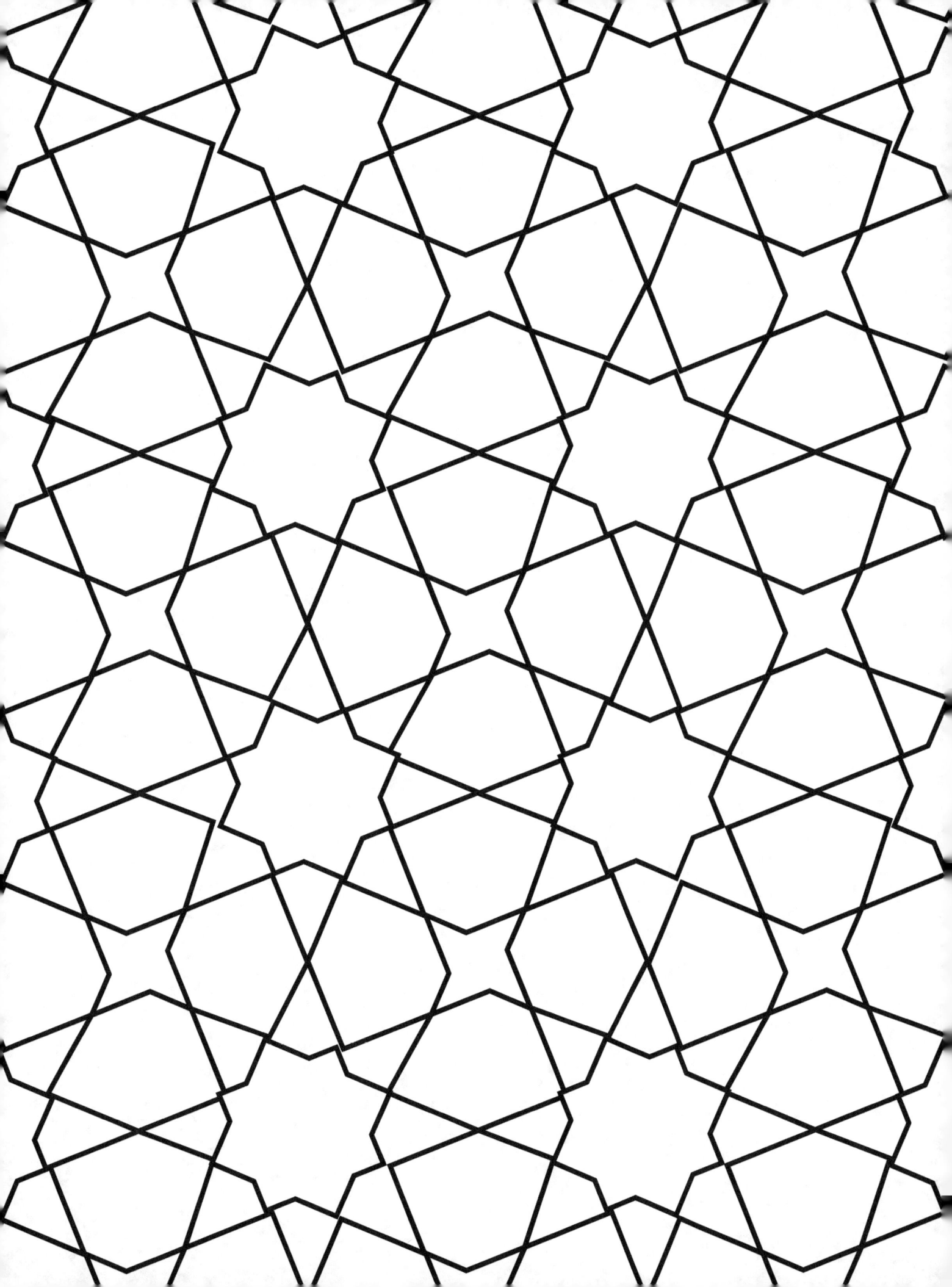

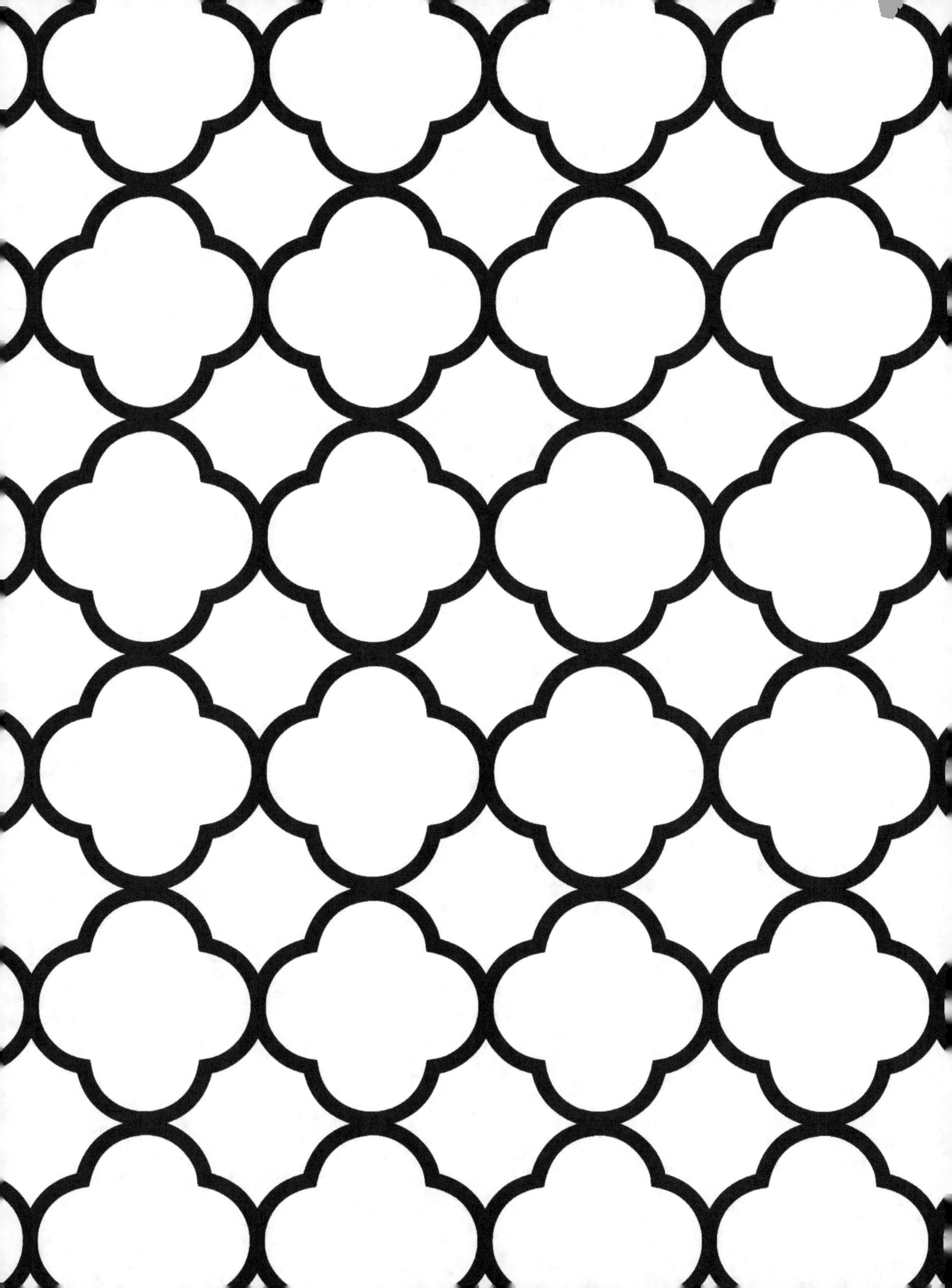

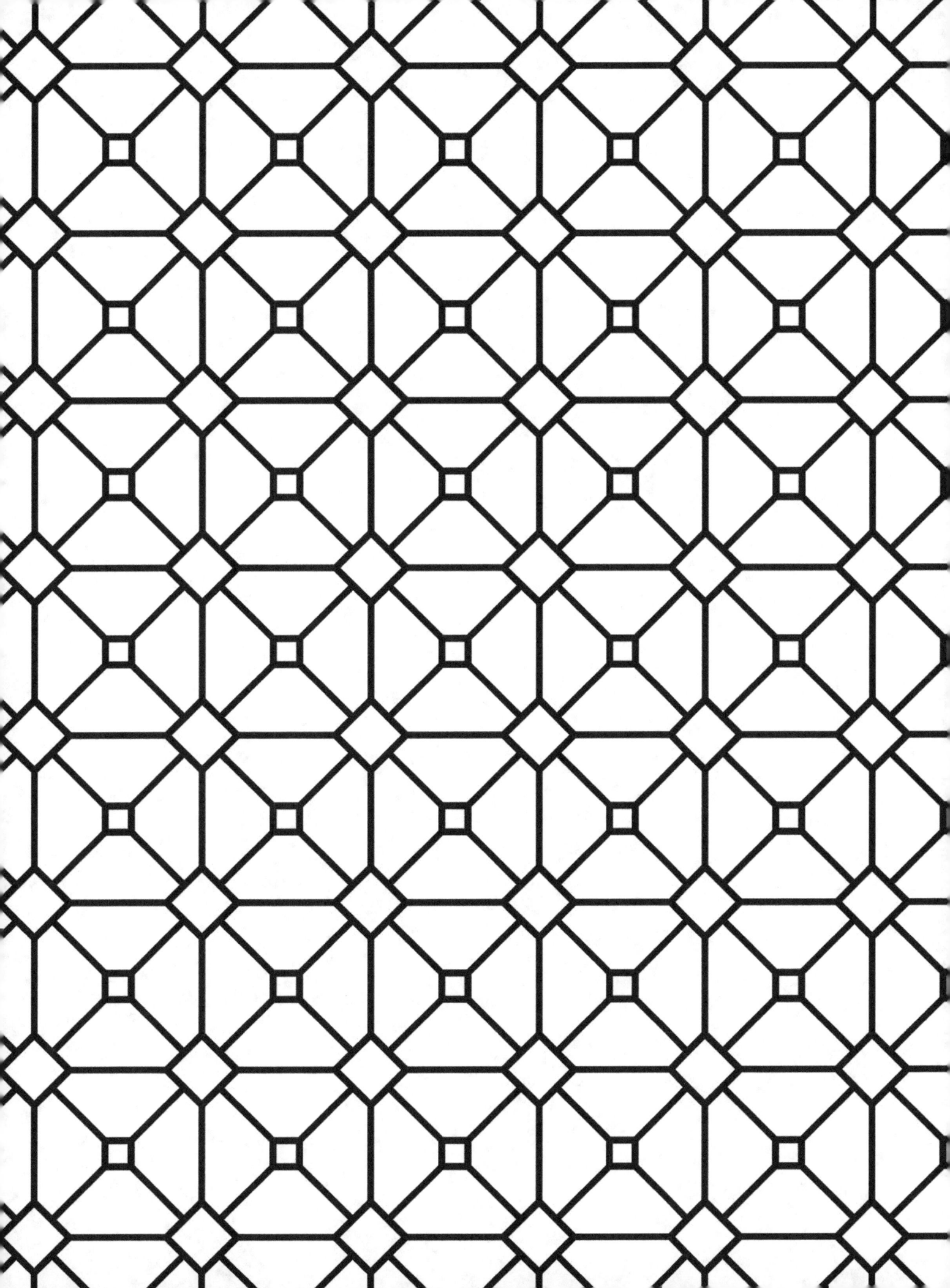

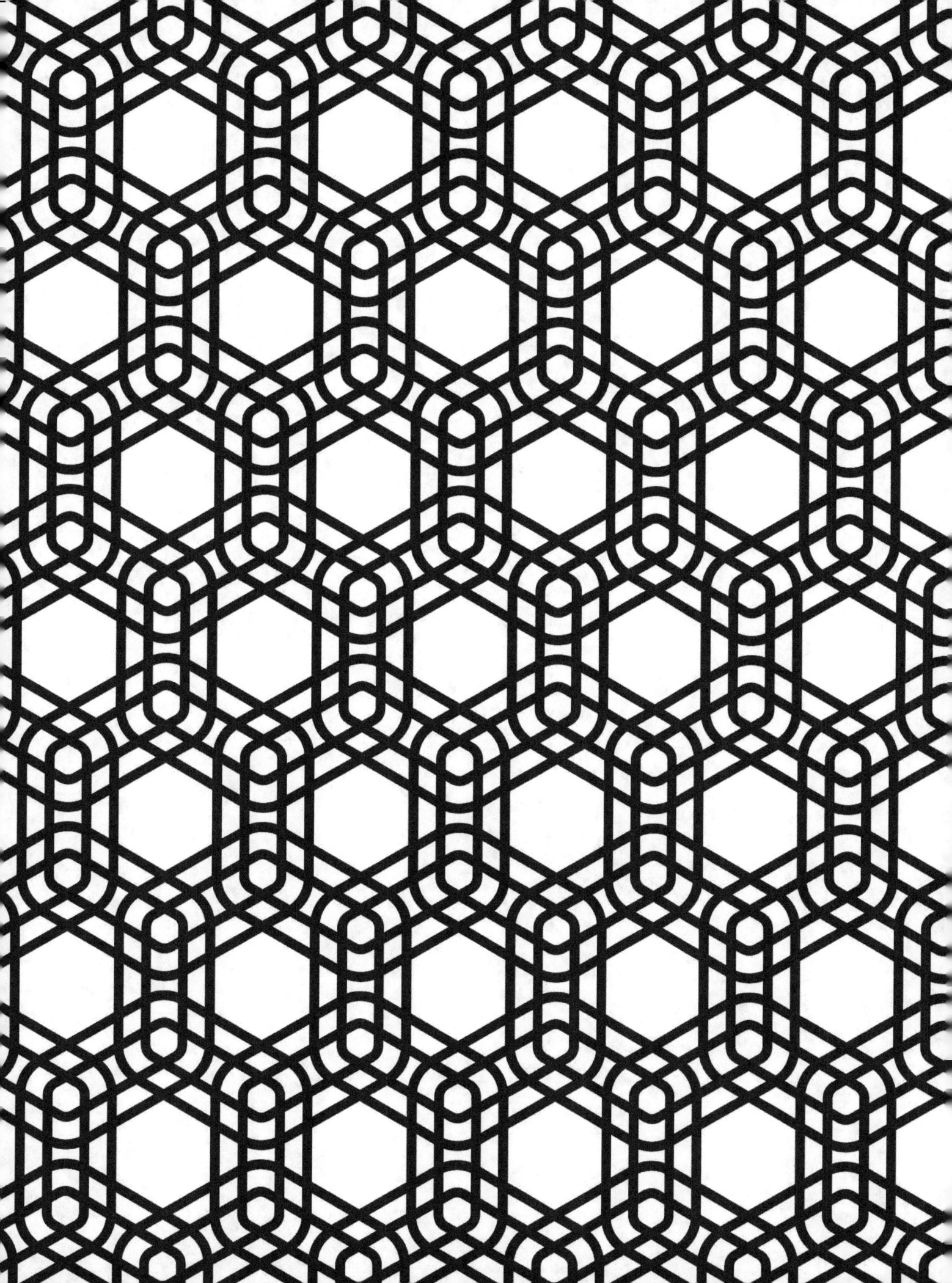

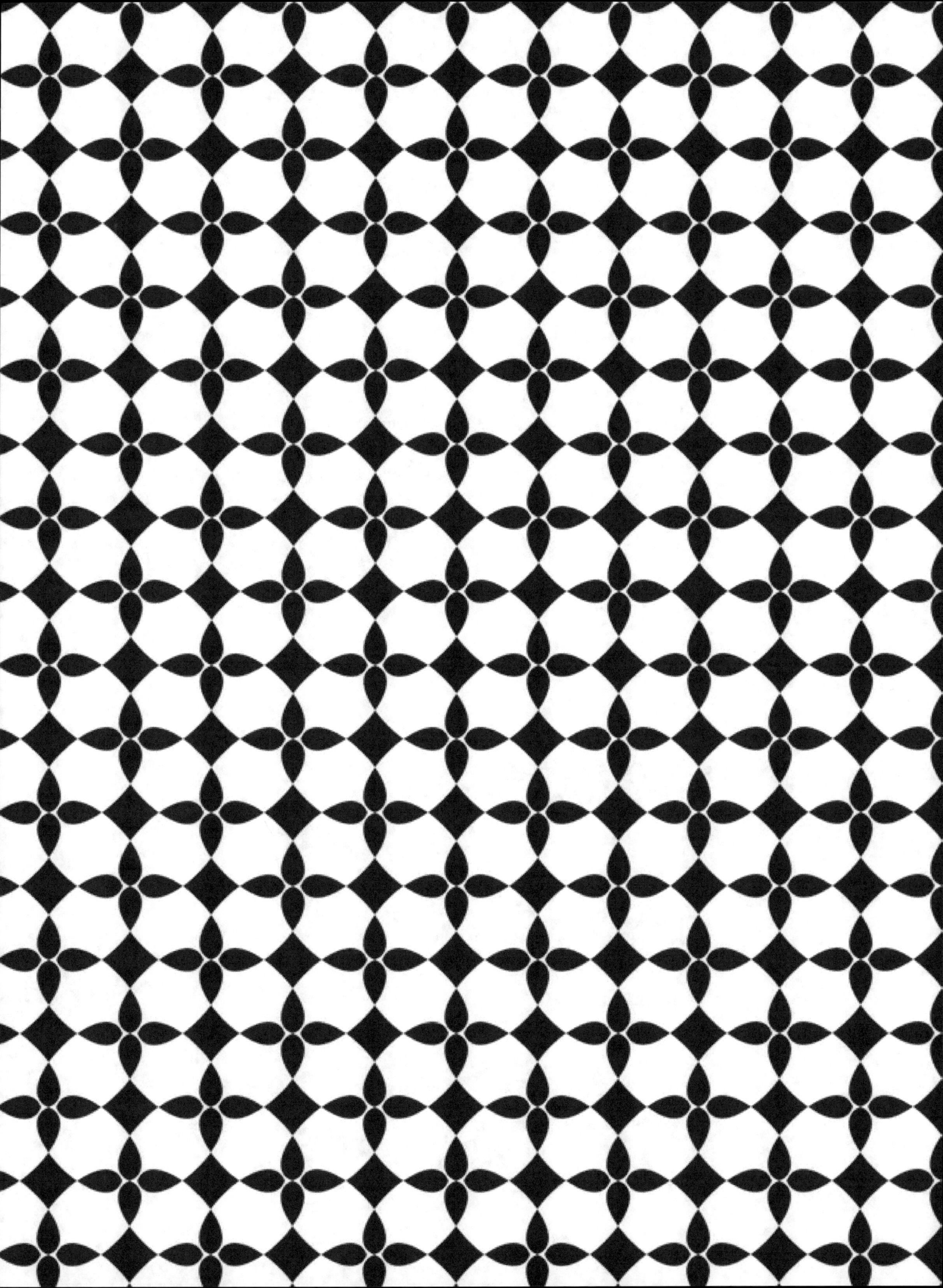

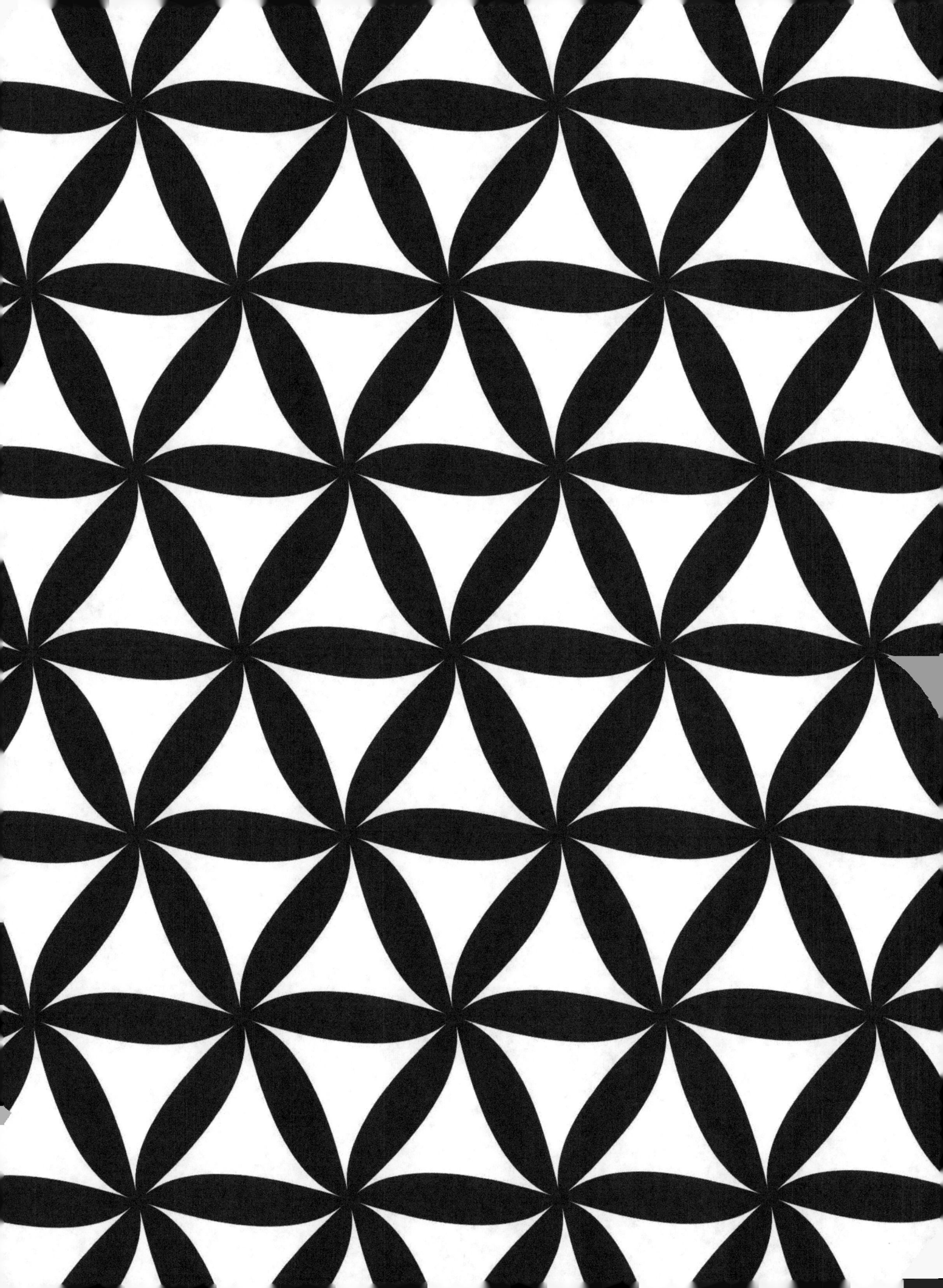

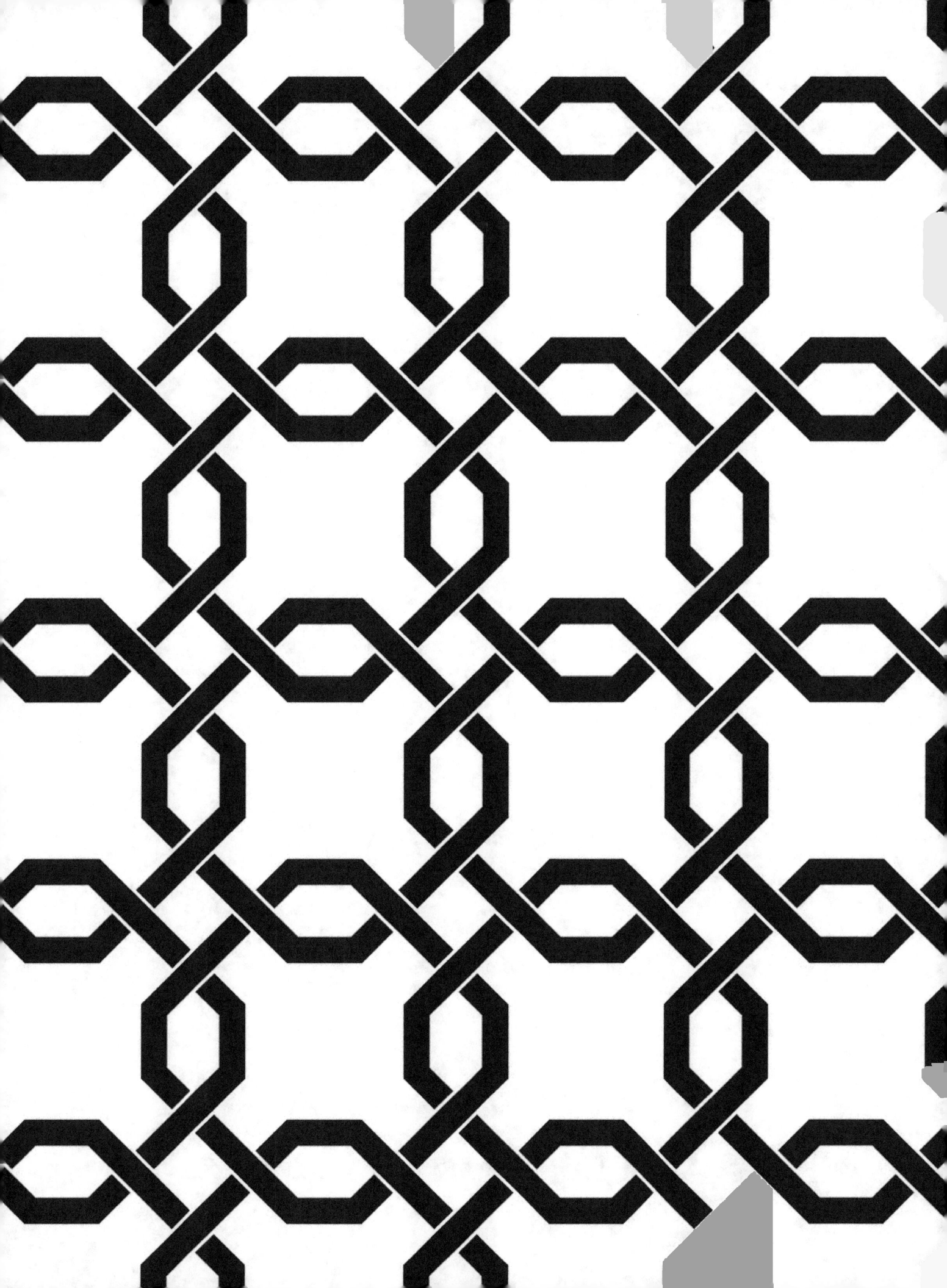

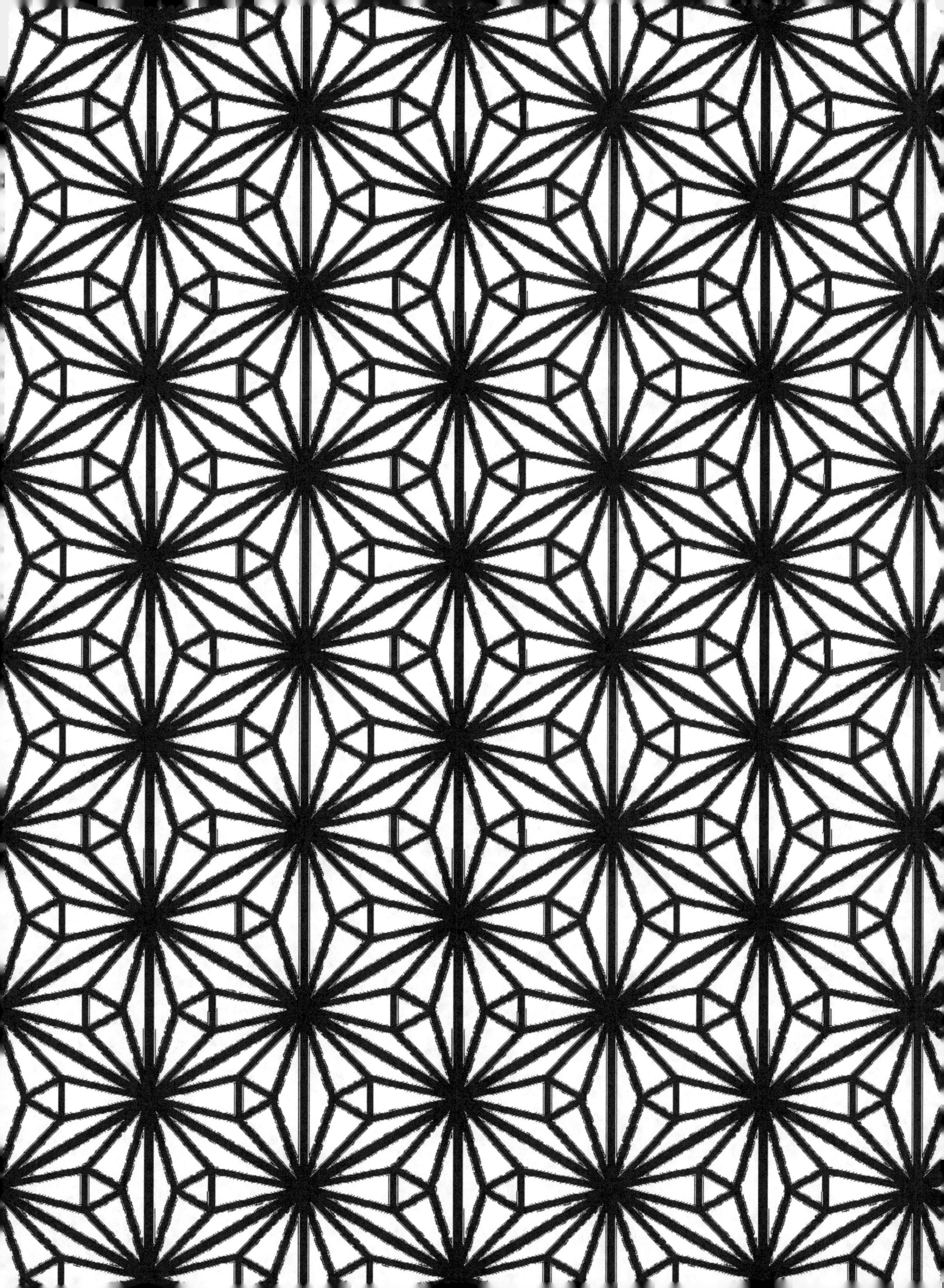

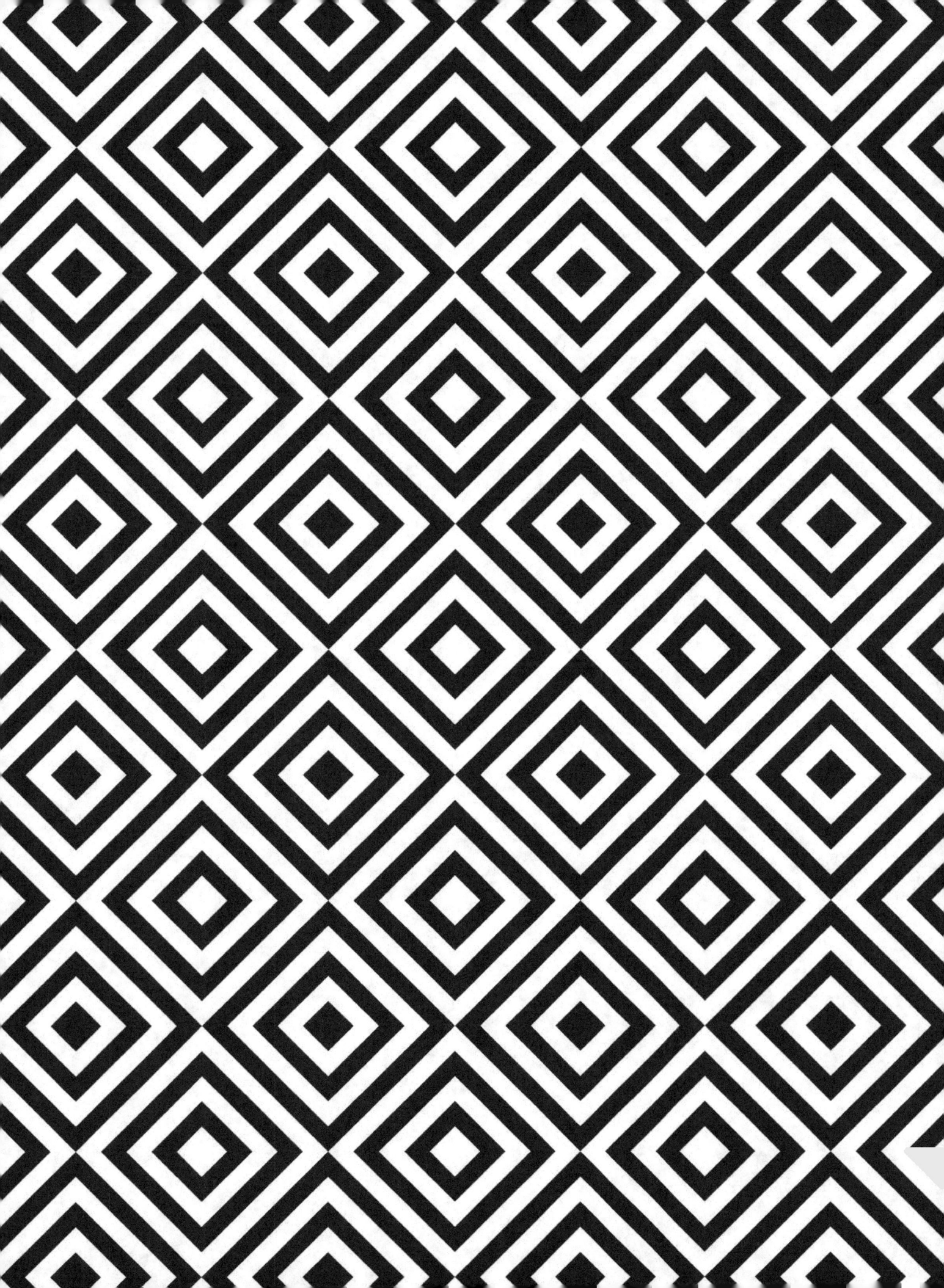

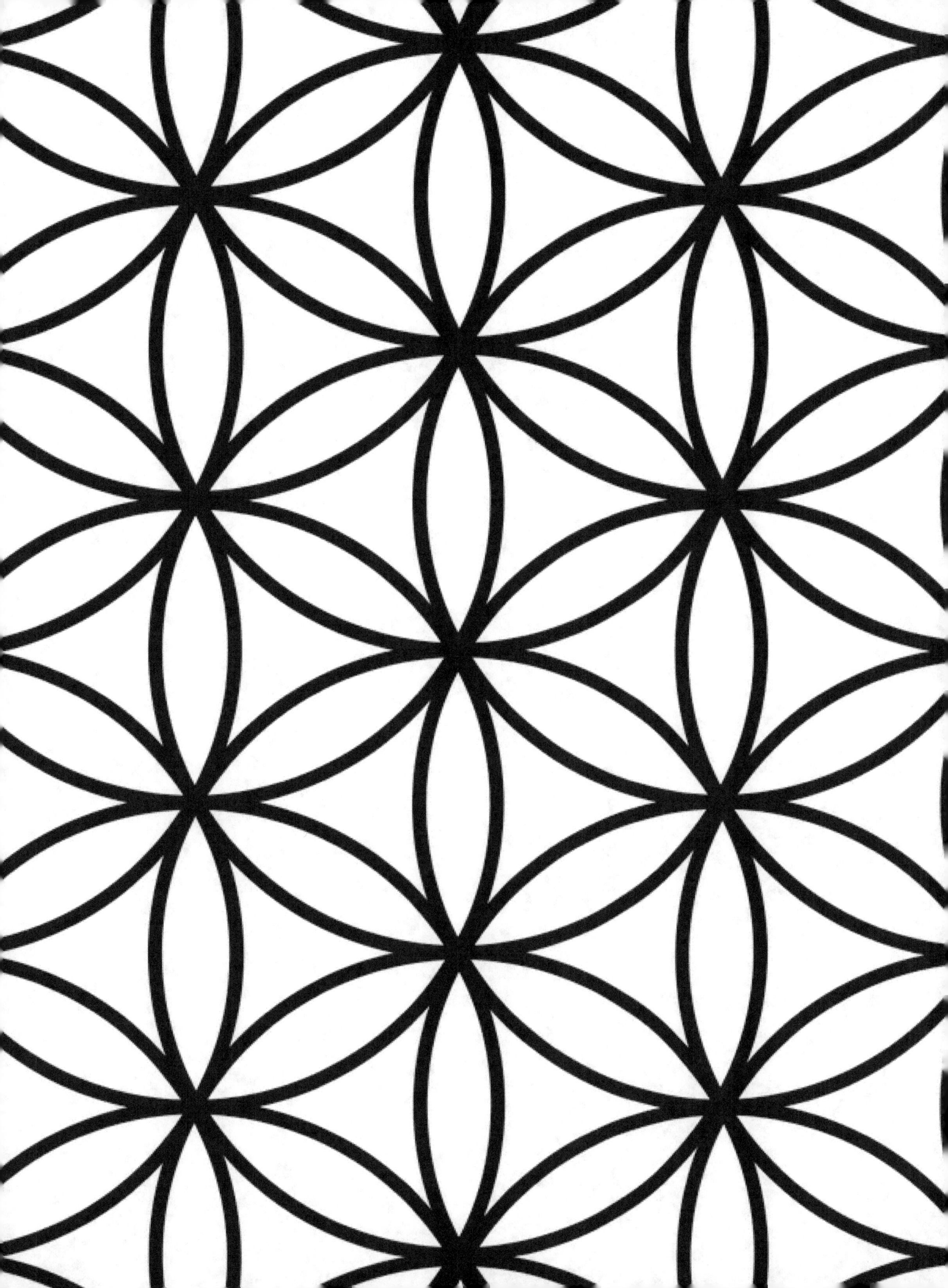

www.ingramcontent.com/pod-product-compliance
Lightning Source LLC
Chambersburg PA
CBHW081703220526
45466CB00009B/2866